How & Why
Birds Use Their Bills

A tern sees danger. It opens its bill wide and calls out a warning.

A sparrow opens its bill and pours out a song.

A bird's bill is its mouth, but it is also a wonderful tool. Birds use their tough, hard bills to grab and eat food, carry things, build nests, clean their feathers, and do many other jobs.

A mallard duck swims in a pond. It dips its bill into the water as it goes. The duck is looking for the tiny water plants and insects that it likes to eat.

Its wide, flat bill acts like a strainer, sorting food from the water. This way of getting food is called dabbling.

The bills of many birds are specially shaped to help the birds eat certain foods. The parrot's hooked bill is a powerful seed cracker. The bill's sharp edges can break open the toughest seed coverings.

The hummingbird has a long, slender bill. This shape is perfect for getting flower nectar, the bird's favorite food. The hummingbird pushes its bill deep into the center of a flower to drink the nectar there.

Birds use their bills to bring food to their young. A robin catches a worm and carries it back to the nest, where the hungry babies wait. The babies open their bills wide to get the meal.

An Atlantic puffin fishes for its family. It catches fish after fish, holding all the fish in its bill. A puffin can carry up to 30 fish at once! The puffin doesn't drop the fish, even when it opens its bill. It uses its tongue to hold the fish against spines in the roof of its mouth.

The puffin's big bill has another special purpose. Its bright colors help the bird attract a mate.

When male puffins go courting, they bob their heads up and down. They almost seem to be showing off their colorful bills. Males and females pair up and get to know each other by rubbing their bills together.

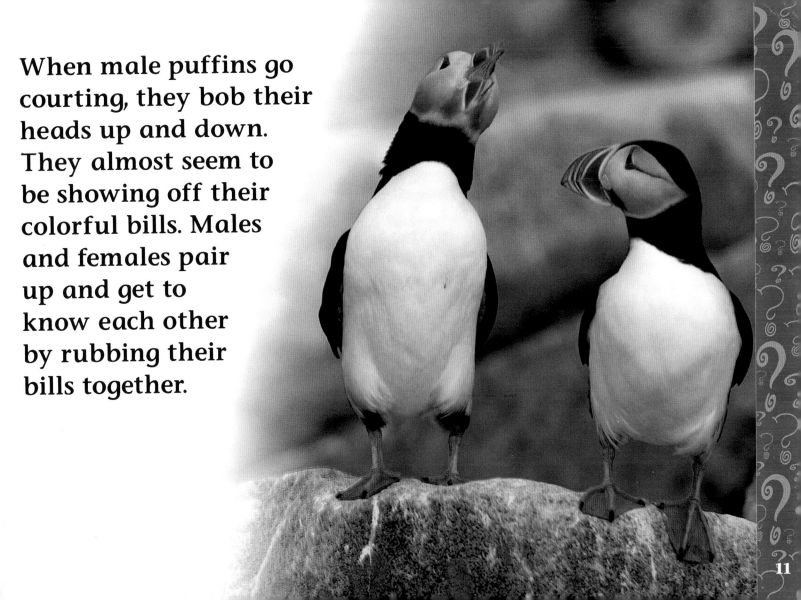

Bills are great tools for building nests. This cedar waxwing has found a piece of thread that is just right for its nest. It holds the thread in its bill and carries the thread to the nest site.

A yellow warbler uses its bill to weave plant fibers into its nest. The fibers make a soft resting place for the bird's eggs.

Birds use their bills for all kinds of jobs. When a tern's egg rolls out of the nest, the bird pushes the egg back in with its bill.

A brown pelican uses its huge bill to preen, or comb, its feathers. All birds preen their feathers this way. Preening is very important. It cleans the feathers and spreads oil over them, keeping them waterproof.

Use the information in this book to answer some "how and why" questions.

- Why does the mallard dip its bill in water?

- How does a hummingbird get nectar?

- How does the puffin carry so many fish at once?

- How do male puffins court?

- How does a yellow warbler use its bill to make a nest?

- Why is preening important for birds?